The
Gospel-Driven
Tongue

LESSONS FROM
JAMES ON
GODLY
CONVERSATION

the
gospel-
driven
tongue

Brian G. Najapfour

FOREWORD BY
GEOFF THOMAS

Reformed
Fellowship Inc.
www.reformedfellowship.net

The Gospel-Driven Tongue

©2017 by Brian G. Najapfour

All rights reserved. No part of this book may be reproduced or transmitted in any form or by any means whatsoever without the prior written permission of the publisher, except in the case of brief quotations embodied in critical articles and reviews. Please refer all pertinent questions to the publisher:

Reformed Fellowship, Inc.
(877) 532–8510
president@reformedfellowship.net

Unless otherwise indicated, all Scripture quotations are from The Holy Bible, English Standard Version, copyright © 2001 by Crossway, a publishing ministry of Good News Publishers. Used by permission. All rights reserved.

Book design by Jeff Steenholdt

ISBN 978-1-935369-13-4

*To my beloved congregation
Dutton United Reformed Church.*

*What a great joy and privilege to
serve God alongside you!*

I am indeed so blessed to be your pastor.

*Thank you for your love
shown to me and my family
in so many ways.*

Contents

Foreword **9**

Preface **13**

1. Be Quick to Hear, But Slow to Speak (James 1:19) **15**

2. Bridle Your Tongue (James 1:26) **26**

3. The Tongue: Small, Yet Great (James 3:2–5a) **37**

4. Seven Descriptions of the Tongue (James 3:5b–8) **45**

5. The Inconsistency of the Tongue (James 3:9–12) **55**

Afterword **66**

About the Author **69**

Foreword

Our words in our homes are to be true and tender. They are to be as loving as were the words of Jesus Christ to his earthly parents (Joseph and Mary) and to their children. His words to his neighbors were also full of love for them. We are to love our neighbors as ourselves—this is the next commandment in importance to loving God with all our hearts—and through our words we can demonstrate our affection. Our words to those who despise us and say all manner of evil against us are to be forgiving, patient, and peace-making words. Remember that a gentle answer will defuse their hot tempers (Prov. 15:1). We are always to speak the truth in love, particularly when we share the gospel of our Lord Jesus Christ.

What we say and how we speak can be a great barometer of the real condition of our hearts, showing whether we are true followers of Jesus or not. How has it been with you? Do your words show that you are Christ's disciple? One of the Ten Commandments tells us not to bear false witness. Do your words preserve and promote truth between one person and another? Do your words maintain the good name of your neighbors? In your daily conversation, do you strive to speak sincerely, telling the truth and nothing but the truth? Do you rejoice in the good name of your neighbors? Do you express your sympathy for those who are in infirmities and sorrows?

Do you keep every promise you have made even to your own hurt? Do you speak only whatsoever is true, honest, just, pure, lovely, and of good report (Phil. 4:8)?

Do you fear that your words might prejudice the truth and the good name of your neighbors? Do you pass an unjust and dismissive judgment on others? Do you call evil good and good evil? Do you conceal the truth? Do you keep silent in a just cause? Do you hold your peace instead of speaking up to reprove evil and then support what is righteous? Do you speak the truth unwisely at the wrong time? Do you lie, slander, backbite, badmouth, and carry tales? Do you scoff and revile? Do you speak harshly and rashly, misconstruing the words of another? Do you speak too highly of yourself and too meanly of others? Do you deny the evident spiritual gifts of God in your fellow believer? Do you aggravate small faults? Do you excuse sins which require a full confession? Do you raise false rumors and promote evil reports? Do you express any grief at the credit that other people receive for their well done work? Do you rejoice in the disgrace of a fellow believer? Do you neglect to do what should be done to deliver a stumbling brother from being blackened by a bad name? Such behavior is not an option for any Christian.

Now, if we are honest with ourselves, we all need help in our speaking. And so, this very readable and helpful book has been written to be read carefully and prayerfully. Indeed, we need to sit under searching ministry and read books such as this one by Pastor Brian Najapfour in which in such a contemporary and compassionate way he shows us how we can change with God's help. After reading this book, may we be more like our Lord Jesus Christ who has saved us and who continues to sanctify our tongues. We really can change as the apostle Peter changed from one who blurted out protestations and falsehoods to one who is a fount of wisdom and exquisite pastoral care. You can change, I can change, and this book, by God's transforming grace, will help us all.

Rev. Geoff Thomas
Alfred Place Baptist Church
Aberystwyth, Wales

Preface

This book has its origin in the pulpit of our congregation, Dutton United Reformed Church. From May 2012 to November 2014 I delivered a series of fifty-five expository sermons on the book of James, and five of these sermons were all about the tongue. With the encouragement of Dan Van Dyke, general manager of *The Outlook* (the journal of Reformed Fellowship, Inc.), I decided to submit the edited version of these five sermons to be published in installments in *The Outlook*. Having received good feedback from the readers, I was inspired to put these articles together as a book. I therefore want to thank all the board members of Reformed Fellowship, Inc., for granting me permission to publish these articles in book format and for agreeing to publish the book itself.

I also wish to express my special thanks to Josh Dear for editing my sermon notes to transform them from sermonic form into book form. I am also indebted to Linda Triemstra for polishing my manuscript and to Jeff Steenholdt for designing and typesetting this book.

A big thanks also goes to my dear wife, Sarah, for helping me improve the manuscript and for her being understanding as I used part of our family time to work on this project. Finally, I am deeply grateful to God for giving me strength to complete this study. To God be the glory!

Chapter 1

Be Quick to Hear, But Slow to Speak

Know this, my beloved brothers: let every person be quick to hear, slow to speak . . .
—James 1:19

Have you ever wondered why God gave us two ears but only one tongue? "Some people say that's because He wanted us to spend twice as much time listening as talking. Others claim it's because He knew listening was twice as hard as talking."[1] Indeed, if we are honest with ourselves, we must admit that listening is not an easy task.

Wives will often ask their husbands, "Will you please just *listen* to me?" Our wives ask this of us men because, when they come to us to share their problem, we immediately speak back to them and try to offer them solutions. In truth, our wives would rather we first take the time to listen to them, giving their concern the serious consideration that it deserves, before formulating a response. Of course, like men, women also struggle at times with their ability to listen well.

James was fully aware of our struggle to listen to others when he wrote, "Know this, my beloved brothers: let every

---

1. Roy B. Zuck, comp., *The Speaker's Quote Book* (Grand Rapids: Kregel, 1997), 231.

person be quick to hear, slow to speak" (James 1:19). As we explore the meaning of this verse in the paragraphs below, we will consider the following three points: the message to which we listen; the motive for which we listen; and the manner by which we listen.

The Message to Which We Listen

In this verse, James specifically addresses his fellow believers in Christ, addressing them as "my beloved brothers." To them, he issues not merely a request but a command—"know this"—which makes it clear that what James is telling them to do is both urgent and crucial. What exactly is it that he wants them to know? Before answering this question, it is helpful to notice a distinction that is made by the King James Version translation of this passage.

In the King James Version, this verse is translated, "Wherefore, my beloved brethren, let every man be swift to hear, slow to speak." The English Standard Version reading begins with the word *know*, and the New International Version expresses this as "take note of this." Therefore, which reading is best?

I favor the King James Version, because the expression "wherefore" seems to offer the most appropriate transition from the preceding verses. In verses 17–18, James writes, "Every good and perfect gift is from above, coming down from the Father of the heavenly lights, who does not change like shifting shadows. He chose to give us birth through the word of truth, that we might be a kind of firstfruits of all he created."[2]

---

2. New International Version.

In verse 17, God is presented as the source of all blessings—the giver of every good and perfect gift. In verse 18, James informs us that one of these gifts which God has given to us is the gift of birth—spiritual birth. Sin gave us death, but God gave us new life in Christ (Eph. 2:1, 4–5), and he chose to accomplish this "through the word of truth." First Peter 1:23 states it this way: "you have been born again, not of perishable seed but of imperishable, through the living and abiding word of God."

In the two previous verses, we have been taught that spiritual birth or regeneration is a gift of God and that God gives this gift through the means of His Word. Given this fact, everyone should *therefore* be quick to listen to "the word of truth." Because Scripture is the primary means through which God gives His marvelous gift of new life in Christ, everyone should be listening to this word of truth, which is the gospel of the Lord Jesus Christ.

What is the object of our listening? It is the very written Word of God—the Bible. Abraham Lincoln once said, "I believe the Bible is the best gift God has ever given to man. All the good from the Savior of the world is communicated to us through this book."[3] It could never be stated strongly enough: we must *listen* to the living Word of God.

The Motive for Which We Listen to God's Word

Why must we listen to God's Word? James gives us five reasons.

---

3. Paul Lee Tan, comp., *Encyclopedia of 7700 Illustrations* (Rockville, MD: Assurance Publishers, 1982), 192.

1. We must listen to God's Word because His Word is His ordinary means by which He saves sinners (James 1:18, 21). Paul confirms this teaching in Romans 10:17: "So faith comes from hearing, and hearing through the word of Christ."

If you are not yet saved, there is good news for you. As you listen to God's Word, God can save you using that Word. Acts 16:31 makes the exhortation plain: "Believe in the Lord Jesus, and you will be saved..." Of course, we are always tempted to ask, "Is that really all that I must do to be saved from my sins?" but James is speaking to us through our text, saying, "Psst! Before you speak . . . LISTEN first! Hear what God's Word says to you, and let this truth sink deeply into your heart!"

Nonetheless, we may want to speak again, asking, "But my sins are too many . . . how can God forgive me?" Again, we should hear the command, "Listen!" and heed biblical teachings such as Isaiah 1:18: "though your sins are like scarlet, they shall be as white as snow." John Newton, writer of the classic hymn "Amazing Grace," when he was old and about to die, said, "My memory is nearly gone, but I remember two things: That I am a great sinner and that Christ is a great Savior."[4] Like Newton, we are great sinners, but we must never forget that Jesus Christ is a great Savior. God's grace is greater than *all* our sins.

2. We also must listen to God's Word because it is the ordinary means by which He sanctifies His people. Why do you think James wrote his book? One of the reasons was to help his fellow believers grow in their faith, even in the midst of trials (James 1:2).

---

4. Kenneth W. Osbeck, *Amazing Grace* (Grand Rapids: Kregel, 2002), 164.

One thing is for sure. We will never mature spiritually if we disregard what the Bible teaches. Instead, we must heed the words of 1 Peter 2:2: "Like newborn infants, long for the pure spiritual milk, that by it you may grow up into salvation." Practically, this means that the gospel must be central in our daily lives.

Some Christians believe that the gospel is only for non-believers. They will say things like, "I no longer need to hear the gospel, because I'm already saved." However, this is the wrong way for believers to think. For example, instructing his fellow believers, Paul says, "Let your manner of life be worthy of the gospel of Christ" (Phil. 1:27). This verse should remind all of us who follow Jesus to keep the gospel ever before us, striving to be continually sanctified by this life-changing gospel.

Of course, our goal is not only to listen to the Bible but to understand and apply it to our lives, as well. A popular children's song expresses this well: "Read your Bible, pray every day. . . . And you'll grow, grow, grow. . . . Don't read your Bible, forget to pray. . . . And you'll shrink, shrink, shrink!" It goes without saying that we should aim for growth in our walk with God, and we can do this only as we spend time feasting upon the rich teaching of God's Word.

3. Another reason for listening to God's Word (and perhaps the most significant reason) is because God *commands* us to do so. The expression "every person" in James 1:19 certainly includes you and me, and the command here is for all of us to be quick to listen to God. When we disregard God's Word, we are both disobeying Him and rejecting anything that He might want to say to us. By neglecting to listen to Him speak

through His Word, we are sinning against God just as surely as if we had disobeyed any other command that He gives to us in Scripture.

There is a growing trend in our churches for young people to bring their smartphones into the worship service and send text messages to friends or play games during the sermon. How offensive this sight must be to our holy God, who desires for every person to hear Him speaking to us through His life-transforming Word! We must pray against this sinful practice, and do all that we can to encourage *every* person—meaning every child, every teenager, every adult, and even every church leader—to listen to God speak through His Word, just as He has instructed us to do.

4. We must also listen to God's Word—the word of truth—because it is literally God's love letter to us. How can we possibly fail to read the loving words which are given to us by our God who loved us so much in Christ? There is no more important person whom we could ever hope to hear from, and there is no excuse that is sufficient for failing to hear God speak to us through His Word.

When I receive a love letter from my wife, I read it with great joy and excitement, because I love her deeply, and I read it multiple times—not out of duty but with delight. After all, who am I, that the woman I love should go to such great lengths to demonstrate her love for me? I feel unworthy of such affection, and thrilled beyond words to receive such a gift from her.

If the loving words of a spouse can bless us in such a way, how much more blessed should we be by God's love letter to us—His holy Word? Remember that James is addressing this book to those who have already received the gift of spiritual birth in their lives. For these born-again people, the voice of their heavenly Father must be so sweet to their ears. This same joy is expressed well in Psalm 119:103: "How sweet are your words to my taste, sweeter than honey to my mouth!"

If you are able to read these same words from James and still not be stirred in your heart toward a deeper knowledge and understanding of God's Word, could it be that perhaps you have not yet experienced God's regenerating grace in your life? If, however, you are confident that you have been born again into God's eternal family, do you desire to hear God speak to you through His Word more than you desire to hear from anyone else in the world? If not, then consider asking God to put such a love for His Word within your heart.

5. Finally, we must listen to God's Word because whenever the Bible is read, taught, or preached, it is *God*, the eternal ruler of heaven and earth, who is ultimately speaking to us. There is no higher authority than God, and we are expected to submit our entire lives to Him. We do this, first, by hearing what He says to us through His Word.

The gospel which is proclaimed to us in Scripture is the gospel of Jesus Christ, the King of kings and the Lord of lords. He is our glorious Savior and Lord, and we must give Him our full attention as we listen to Him teaching us through His Word—the Word which the Father, the Son, and the Holy Spirit have given to us so that we might know our triune God more fully.

Ironically, we all want God to listen to us when we pray, but we rarely want to listen to Him when He speaks to us through His Word. As we remember that it is God who speaks to us through the Bible, it should motivate us to listen far more attentively to what it says.

The Manner by Which We Listen

Given the importance of our listening to God's Word, in what manner should we do this? There are many things that we could say about this, of course, but a helpful guide for us at this point is the Westminster Larger Catechism, which asks: "What is required of those that hear the word preached?" (Q 160). Answer: "It is required of those that hear the word preached, that they attend upon it with diligence (Prov. 8:34), preparation (1 Peter 2:1–2; Luke 8:18), and prayer (Ps. 119:18; Eph. 6:18–19)."[5] To express this wise counsel in a slightly different way, we must strive to be diligent, disciplined, and dependent upon God as we grow in our submission to His Word.

1. We must be *diligent* in listening to God's Word. By nature we do not want to listen to God. In our natural condition, we are like our first parents, Adam and Eve, who did not pay attention to God's commandment. However, God calls us to listen to His Word with all diligence. As our text instructs, we should "be quick" to hear God speaking to us—making every effort to become good listeners in our churches and eager students of the Word in our homes. Let us, therefore, pray and ask God to put a hunger for His Word within us, and to help us grow in the ability to listen well to the preaching and teaching of His Word.

---

5 *Westminster Larger Catechism* (1647) in *Reformed Confessions of the 16th and 17th Centuries in English Translation: Volume 4, 1600–1693*, compiled with introductions by James T. Dennison (Grand Rapids: Reformation Heritage Books, 2010), 341.

2. We must also be *disciplined* in preparing ourselves to meet with God regularly, both in public worship, with our brothers and sisters in Christ, and in our own daily quiet times with the Lord. We must realize that the devil will do all that he can to distract us from listening to God's Word, and we must make every effort to stay faithful in the time that we spend with God and His Word. Spending time with God must be the top priority of our lives. Every opportunity to meet with God in prayer, in the reading of His Word, or in corporate worship with His people must be treated as sacred. A half-hearted effort will never be enough to keep us growing in our walk with God. We must keep God first in our lives and refuse to let the enemy keep us from meeting with Him.

3. In the end, though, we must also recognize that we are still completely *dependent* upon God, even in our quest to grow closer to Him. No matter how hard we try to keep God first in our lives, the sin with which we still struggle will always prevent us from being perfect Christians. Oh, how dependent we are upon God's grace and mercy in every area of our lives!

Despite our greatest efforts, we will never be as diligent as we should in our reading of Scripture, in our prayer life, in our church attendance, or in any other area of spiritual growth. We should always continue to work toward increased growth in our walk with the Lord, but there will never be a time when we don't continue to need His divine help.

Recognizing our dependence upon God, let us be in the habit of praying before, during, and after our times of Bible study, asking the Lord to speak to us through the text, to open our minds to what it is saying to us, to show us how to meditate on it properly and to apply it effectively to our lives. As we come to worship with our church family, we should also ask God to help us listen well to what is preached, to bless the preacher as well as all who will hear him preach, and to remove any distractions that might hinder us from hearing God speak to us through His Word.

There once was a man who traveled to different places selling individual books from the Bible. One night, as he was passing through a forest in Sicily, he was stopped by a robber who demanded that he burn all the books that he had— the books of the Bible. After starting the fire, the traveling salesman asked if he might be allowed to read a small portion from each book before surrendering them to the flames. The thief agreed to the request.

The man began to read passages such as Psalm 23, the Sermon on the Mount, the parable of the Good Samaritan, and 1 Corinthians 13. After each excerpt was read, the outlaw exclaimed, "That's a good book! We won't burn that. Give it to me." None of the books were burned, but all were taken by the thief. Some years later, the robber appeared again, but now as an ordained Christian minister. God used the Bible to transform this robber into a servant of the Lord Jesus Christ.[6]

I'm fully convinced that God's Word is living, active, and powerful. Through His Word, God transforms lives. What all of us must do, therefore, is listen to God's Word, and hear God speaking to us through it.

---

6. I owe this illustration to Zuck, *The Speaker's Quote Book*, 26.

Study Questions

1. Why must we listen to God's Word?

2. In what way do we still need the gospel if we are already Christians?

3. What are some things that might hinder us from hearing God speak to us through His Word?

4. Do you listen attentively to the preaching and teaching of God's Word? Are you quick to listen and slow to speak?

5. Do you pray before, during, and after listening to God's message? Do you also remember the preacher or teacher of God's Word in your prayer?

6. How can we continue to grow in our love for God's Word? Can we say with the psalmist, "Oh how I love your law! It is my meditation all the day" (Ps. 119:97)?

Chapter 2

Bridle Your Tongue

If anyone thinks he is religious and does not bridle his tongue but deceives his heart, this person's religion is worthless.
—James 1:26

In the previous chapter, I sought to show what it means to be "slow to speak" according to God's Word. Guarding our speech, though, requires that we learn how to control the use of our tongues for God's glory. In this chapter, I will offer three biblical reasons why we must control our tongues, followed by three practical suggestions regarding how we may do so.

Three Reasons Why We Must Control Our Tongues

1. If we do not control our tongues, we deceive ourselves.

Since the book of James was written specifically to Christians, it is worth noting that the word *anyone* at the start of James 1:26 does not exclude faithful, growing Christians. On the contrary, it suggests that every person who professes faith in Christ should receive and heed the warning which follows. However, James is particularly describing a person who has convinced himself that he is religious—someone who is not genuinely submitted to Christ but who outwardly performs most or all of the expected activities of the Christian life.

This sort of person is likely to be active in attending church, generous in giving, quick to volunteer to serve others, and involved in evangelism, missions, choir, or virtually any other aspect of a church's ministry. Someone fitting this description could conceivably be a deacon, an elder, a Bible teacher, a missionary, or even, in some cases, a pastor. Yet, to a person who is externally religious, James warns, "You may believe yourself to be a religious person, but if you do not bridle your tongue, you deceive your heart!"

As you may know, a bridle is a device that fits on a horse's head for the purpose of controlling and guiding the horse. The bridle enables riders to steer horses away from danger and toward the proper path. In this verse, James is using the term *bridle* as a verb, to emphasize strongly the need for every Christian to guide, guard, and restrain our speech. In fact, James warns readers that if we don't do this, we are deceiving ourselves concerning our relationship with Christ.

So, if there is a local church member who is active in the life of the church but who consistently slanders, backbites, and spreads gossip about others, then it is likely, according to James, that this person has deceived himself into thinking that he belongs to Christ when he does not. People in this situation need to stop flattering themselves and believing themselves to be better than they are, and instead examine their hearts sincerely before the Lord.

By the way, we always need to be extremely cautious of people who try to spread gossip to us, because the same person who is willing to gossip to us will also surely be willing to gossip about us.

It can be tricky, though, when the people who behave this way profess to be fellow Christians, because they will often share idle gossip about others disguised as prayer requests—sometimes even verbally attacking someone and then asking us to pray for them to change in some significant way. When this happens, we need to learn to say to the gossipers, "Thank you for sharing this information with me, but that's not the kind of information that I need to hear about from you."

We should also recognize that the sin addressed in our text can be demonstrated in a variety of ways. It can be practiced by children who knowingly tell lies to their parents or to others, or by parents who regularly use abusive words when they discipline their children. Parents—we must always be careful to use words which will help and not hurt our children! The "anyone" in this passage may also refer to a wife or a husband who uses hateful words to respond to marital conflict. No marriage is perfect, but when there are problems and disagreements, we must be intentional about handling them in God-honoring ways.

James is reminding us, though, that while it is always good to do Christ-honoring things such as attending church regularly and actively serving others, such practices tell us little about what is truly in a person's heart. A person's speech, more than outward practices, can serve as a more accurate barometer of what is happening in a person's heart and of where that person stands in his relationship with God.

So, what should we learn from our passage? Here, James is calling us to examine ourselves sincerely. If people claim to be believers in Christ but do not bridle their tongue by speaking in ways that honor God, they deceive themselves and need to examine earnestly their own heart, ultimately acknowledging this sinful behavior that they practice and repenting of it before the Lord. The people who are currently in this situation are not being told by God that they are truly His, but rather they deceive themselves into believing that they do, though their assumptions about their own spiritual well-being are false. Search your hearts, my friends!

Paul writes in Galatians 6:3–4, "For if anyone thinks he is something, when he is nothing, he deceives himself. But let each one test his own work." God expects us to test, or examine, our own behavior to see if it matches the behavior of a true child of God. In a similar way, Ephesians 5:4 exhorts us, "Let there be no filthiness nor foolish talk nor crude joking [among you]." If we belong to Christ, both our words and our actions must be notably different from those who remain outside of Christ.

To be more precise, James warns that the person who fails to bridle his tongue "deceives his heart"—as in, his own heart, even more so than the hearts of others. It is bad enough to deceive people and to cause others to be hurt by our speech, but this verse reminds us that by doing this, we are causing the greatest harm to ourselves, as we consistently offend God with our speech while pretending He is pleased with us.

People who claim to belong to Christ but use their words to harm others prove themselves to be liars, cheaters, and hypocrites. They hear God's Word being taught, and are likely familiar with the ninth commandment, which commands that "you shall not bear false witness against your neighbor" (Exod. 21:16). Yet, they still use their words to destroy the lives of others.

We should acknowledge that all of us have been guilty of sinning in this way at times. We have used our tongues to praise God on Sunday, but then used the same tongues to curse others at other times. We have been worshipers on Sunday and then gossipers on Monday. However, God wants us to examine ourselves on this matter, to ask sincerely whether we have sinned with our speech, and to commit, by His grace, to change for the better.

2. If we do not control our tongue, we damage our religion, which is biblical Christianity.

When people fail to bridle their tongues and are deceived about their own devotion to Christ, James teaches, "this person's religion is worthless." By failing to guard our speech, we can permanently destroy our public witness for Christ. The people who hear our sinful speech will either believe that we do not belong to God or else they will wrongfully accuse God of being responsible for our sinfulness. God-honoring speech reflects the "religion that is pure and undefiled before God" (James 1:27), which God calls us to live out, but an unbridled tongue can publicly defile that very religion.

Lost sinners will certainly not be drawn nearer to Christ by our unholy speech but are more likely to be pushed further away from Him. Consider how easily ungodly speech can cause damage in the work environment. When an employee frequently curses, lies, argues, tells vulgar jokes, or speaks harshly to others, it is common for the other employees to question his character. If it becomes known that the ungodly employee claims to be a Christian and attends a particular church, what will the other employees be left to believe about God and about the church that he attends? Many non-believers have been discouraged from following Christ because of situations like this, reasoning "If that's what Christianity looks like, I want nothing to do with it!"

Even the name of Jesus can be damaged (in an earthly sense) by our sinful behavior, because when we claim to be Christians, we carry His name with us wherever we go. People who know us, and who know that we profess to be Christians, will hear our ungodly talk and believe that our speech must be typical of those who belong to Christ. Worse yet, they might even presume to blame Jesus for our ungodly speech and actions, believing our behavior to be a result of His teaching and authority in our lives. How can we possibly bring such shame upon our blessed Savior's name?

Why is it that the sin of an uncontrolled tongue is singled out here as the one which could render a person's religion "worthless"? James, under the inspiration of the Holy Spirit, highlights this sin because the Bible takes this kind of sin very seriously! It is a really big deal in Scripture, because, again, our speech is an indicator of our spirituality. What you say is reflection of what you think and what you feel. That's why, in Matthew 12:34, Jesus says, "How can you speak good, when you are evil? For out of the abundance of the heart the mouth speaks."

I remember talking to a lady who was born in the Netherlands but has lived in the United States for many years. She was a bit disappointed that whenever she speaks in English she still has a Dutch accent. I said to her, "Please don't be disappointed with your accent, because it's an indicator of your identity." I asked, "Are you not proud of your Dutch heritage?" She replied, "You're right. I should be proud of my heritage."

When I speak in English, which is not my first language, people hear my accent and recognize that I am not originally from the United States. As Christians, we have become citizens of heaven. Now, whenever we speak, people around us should be able to hear our "heavenly accent." Do they? Are we ever asked, "Where are you really from?" Do we speak in a way that reflects our Lord and our true eternal home?

In Colossians 4:5–6, the apostle Paul admonishes us, "Walk in wisdom toward outsiders, making the best use of the time. Let your speech always be gracious, seasoned with salt, so that you may know how you ought to answer each person." God expects us to bring this area of our lives under submission to Him—looking to Jesus Christ as the ultimate example of how we should speak and trusting in the Holy Spirit to transform our hearts and lives increasingly into the likeness of Christ.

3. If we do not control our tongues, we destroy ourselves.

If we willfully and deliberately let our tongues go unguarded, it is like riding a horse with no bridle or driving a car with no steering wheel. In either case, we are sure to cause great harm to ourselves, as well as to others. Failing to bridle our tongues, though, is just as dangerous.

A number of Bible passages affirm this point, including the following:

   a. The mouth of the righteous brings forth wisdom, but the perverse tongue will be cut off. (Prov. 10:31)
   b. Whoever guards his mouth preserves his life; he who opens wide his lips comes to ruin. (Prov. 13:3)
   c. Whoever desires to love life and see good days, let

him keep his tongue from evil and his lips from
speaking deceit. (1 Pet. 3:10)

Someone once said, "Gossip not only hurts others, it can
also boomerang and hurt the one who starts it."[7] If you are a
gossiper, do not think that you will not be hurt by what you
do, for by not controlling your tongue, you are destroying
both yourself and others.

Three Biblical Exhortations

So, what should we do in response to the warnings given in
James 1:26? Here are three biblical exhortations which we
should be especially careful to heed.

1. Get down on your knees and pray to God.

In this passage of Scripture, James is not only addressing
other people; he is speaking to you and to me, as well. We
should all be deeply convicted by this passage of Scripture,
because all of us have failed in this area at times. We are
guilty before God of sinning with our speech, and we should
want to do all that we can to avoid sinning in this way again.

So, with that in mind, we should readily confess our sinful
use of the tongue to God, not denying it, making excuses for
it, or attempting to justify it in any way. Instead, we should be
honest with God about the ways that we have failed Him and
caused others to be hurt, and earnestly seek His forgiveness,
asking the Spirit of God to help us guard our speech in the
days to come.

We should pray with King David in Psalm 141:3: "Set a
guard, O Lord, over my mouth; keep watch over the door of

---

7. Roy B. Zuck, comp., *The Speaker's Quote Book* (Grand Rapids:
Kregel, 1997), 176.

my lips!" In a similar manner, we can sing the lyrics of one of the great hymns:

> Take my life, and let it be consecrated, Lord, to Thee.
> Take my voice, and let me sing always, only, for my King.
> Take my lips, and let them be filled with messages from Thee.

2. Guard your tongue.

Of course, we must become increasingly intentional about doing precisely what this biblical text warns us to do—guarding our tongues. However, we must also remember that we cannot do this in our own strength, but only with God's help will we be able to succeed in this challenging but crucial task.

Some additional Bible verses which can serve as helpful reminders to us include the following:

d. I will guard my ways, that I may not sin with my tongue; I will guard my mouth with a muzzle. (Ps. 39:1)

e. Keep your tongue from evil and your lips from speaking deceit. (Ps. 34:13)

f. Let no corrupting talk come out of your mouths, but only such as is good for building up, as fits the occasion, that it may give grace to those who hear. (Eph. 4:29)

These verses, and others like them which remind us to guard our speech, should become increasingly familiar to us. Even a beloved children's song can help remind us to guard our words in a way that honors the Lord:

> O, be careful little mouth what you say;
> O, be careful little mouth what you say;

There's a Father up above
And He's looking down in love;
So, be careful little mouth what you say.

Some people have even found the following acronym for THINK to be a helpful tool in this journey:

T – Is it true?
H – Is it helpful?
I – Is it inspiring?
N – Is it necessary?
K – Is it kind?

In any case, we should always strive to use our tongues for God's glory and for the edification of his church, and ask the Holy Spirit to assist us with this task.

3. Go to Jesus Christ.

As in every other area of our lives, we are to keep looking to Jesus as our ultimate example and working to imitate the way He lived during His earthly life. First Peter 2:21–23 serves as a strong reminder in this regard: "For to this you have been called, because Christ also suffered for you, leaving you an example, so that you might follow in his steps. He committed no sin, neither was deceit found in his mouth. When he was reviled, he did not revile in return; when he suffered, he did not threaten, but continued entrusting himself to him who judges justly."

So, again, we must determine to make guarding our speech a high priority in our lives, since by doing so we will demonstrate our genuine faithfulness to God and our true concern for the well-being of others as well as ourselves. God shows us, through the Spirit-inspired writings of James, that an unbridled tongue is a serious sin which should not be practiced by the people of God. Let us respond appropriately by receiving this instruction from God's Word and speaking only words through which Christ will be glorified.

Study Questions

1. What does sinful speech reveal about the true condition of our hearts?

2. How is Christ's reputation in the world affected by the words and actions of His followers?

3. What should you say to a person who gossips to you?

4. How can sinful speech lead to our own destruction?

5. What does it mean to seek to have a "heavenly accent"?

6. Do you speak in a way that shows that you are a Christian?

Chapter 3

The Tongue: Small, Yet Great

For we all stumble in many ways. And if anyone does not stumble in what he says, he is a perfect man, able also to bridle his whole body. If we put bits into the mouths of horses so that they obey us, we guide their whole bodies as well. Look at the ships also: though they are so large and are driven by strong winds, they are guided by a very small rudder wherever the will of the pilot directs. So also the tongue is a small member, yet it boasts of great things. —James 3:2–5a

According to researchers at the University of Arizona, "men talk just as much as women—on average, 16,000 words in a day."[1] Imagine that . . . sixteen thousand words in a day! However, Proverbs 10:19 warns, "When words are many, transgression is not lacking." Indeed, the more you talk, the more likely you sin. Aware of the teaching found in this verse, it is no wonder that James takes the time to write about taming the tongue. As we reflect on James 3:2–5a, there are at least three significant observations that we should make: the inclusive truth about the tongue, the importance of the tongue, and the inclination of the tongue.

---

1. Ashley Phillips, "Study: Women Don't Talk More Than Men," ABC News, July 5, 2007, http://abcnews.go.com/Technology/story?id=3348076&page=1 (accessed June 6, 2016).

The Inclusive Truth about the Tongue

First, we must recognize the inclusive (or universal) truth about the tongue, which is that we all make moral mistakes with it. Verse 2 reminds us that "we all stumble." In this context, "stumble" means to fall into sin and commit moral error. You and I—all of us—struggle and fall into sin at times with our tongues. The text adds that we do this "in many ways." This can include such sinful behavior as lying, slander, gossip, vulgarity, insults, blasphemous comments, and verbally abusing others. Indeed, one of the many ways in which we sin against God is in our speech, and there are so many ways in which we are liable to do this.

James continues, "And if anyone does not stumble in what he says"—that is to say, if anyone claims to have mastered the use of his tongue—"he is a perfect man." In other words, to say that you never sin in your speech is to declare boldly that you never sin—that you are perfect. Anyone who fits this description is "able also to bridle his whole body." Supposedly, this person is "perfect" in the sense that he is able to control all parts of his body. But the truth is that nobody is perfect.

To insist that you have fully mastered the use of your tongue is to imply that you are fully perfect, which means, also, that you have absolute control over your mind, your eyes, your heart, and so on. But the fact that you sometimes stumble in what you say shows that you also stumble at times in other ways. Without doubt, we all stumble in regard to our mind (what we think), our eyes (what we see), our ears (what we hear), our heart (what we feel), our hands (what we do), and our feet (where we go).

We all stumble, we are all vulnerable to temptation, and we all sin. Even James acknowledges his own need to admit this. He intentionally uses the pronoun "we," counting himself among those who fail in their moral behavior. Proverbs 20:9 asks, "Who can say, 'I have made my heart pure; I am clean from my sin'?" Who among us no longer falls into temptation? Not one person! This truth is a universal one: we still struggle with sin, and this includes sin with regard to our tongue.

Children, have you spoken to your parents disrespectfully? Have you lied to them? If you know that you have done this, will you now come before the Lord and repent of your sin, and commit yourself to speaking to your parents with love and respect?

Parents, have you used overly harsh words when disciplining your children? Have you ever said things that you did not truly mean, such as, "You are always bad!" (knowing that your child is not always bad), or "You don't do anything right!" (knowing that it is not true)? If you have, will you confess your error to your children, seek their forgiveness for this, and repent before God?

Husbands and wives, have you communicated with one another in anger when there have been disagreements between you? Have you used unnecessary yelling to communicate with one another? Worse yet, have you done this in front of your children? Do you need to confess sin of this sort to one another—and to God—in order to restore health, happiness, and love to your marriage? If so, then is it not worth the effort to do this in order to see the joy and blessing increase in your home?

Proverbs 12:18 says, "Thoughtless words can wound as deeply as any sword, but wisely spoken words can heal."[2] Oh, friends, how often have we deeply wounded other people because we were not careful with our speech? Far too often, we are hasty, careless, insensitive, and thoughtless of the ways that we speak to others. We should take this matter seriously, for we all stumble in what we say, and this truth is inclusive, as James tells us.

The Importance of the Tongue

Second, we should acknowledge the importance of the tongue, which is great. James already addressed this subject in James 1:26, where he wrote, "If anyone thinks he is religious and does not bridle his tongue but deceives his heart, this person's religion is worthless." Now, in chapter 3, James delves more deeply into this problem, offering us twelve additional verses of instruction about our speech. The fact that he is teaching us about the tongue in multiple parts of his epistle should leave no doubt concerning the subject's importance to James—and, more especially, to God.

Clearly, the tongue is an important part of our bodies. We should note, though, that James sometimes uses the word *tongue* in a literal sense to mean a physical part of our bodies, while in other verses he uses the word figuratively, in regard to our speech and our communication with one another. In regard to our physical bodies, the tongue is vital. There are certain parts of our bodies, such as our wisdom teeth, our tonsils, and our appendix, which can be removed with little

---

2. Good News Translation.

consequence. However, without a tongue, we would have great difficulty communicating with other people.

James is drawing the conclusion that the tongue, though small, can greatly affect the outcome of our lives. He offers two illustrations to help us see this. First, he likens the tongue to the bit in the mouth of a horse (v. 3). That small metal mouthpiece, when put on a horse, is what enables a rider to steer the direction of the horse. Without the bit, a rider can have great difficulty controlling where the horse goes. In the same way, each of us must control our tongue, which in turn helps determine the direction in which our life goes.

The popular commentator Albert Barnes once wrote, "A man always has complete government over himself if he has the entire control of his tongue. It is that by which he gives expression to his thoughts and passions; and if that is kept under proper restraint, all the rest of his members are as easily controlled as the horse is by having the control of the bit."[3] This, of course, is true.

As a second illustration, James compares the tongue with the rudder of a ship (v. 4). What a powerful illustration this is. In fact, James made excellent use of illustrations throughout his epistle, a skill which he, no doubt, acquired from listening to his half-brother, Jesus, when He taught. Illustrations are intended to help us learn profound truths about God, and that is precisely what James is aiming to do here. He is explaining that even ships, which are large and are constantly being blown to and fro by the wind, are guided by the small rudder

---

3. Albert Barnes, *Notes, Explanatory and Practical, on the General Epistles of James, Peter, John and Jude* (New York: Harper & Brothers, 1850), 65.

and by the will of the captain, who controls the rudder and determines the ship's direction.

To control a ship's rudder is to control the ship. Again, we see the same principle being taught. While the tongue is a small part of our bodies, how we use it can greatly influence the direction of our entire lives. None of us are perfect, and we will all continue to struggle with temptation regarding our speech. But the more control that each of us has over our tongue, the more control that we will have regarding the direction of our lives.

Throughout his book, James is concerned that some people claim to be Christians but demonstrate no good works. They give no signs or evidence that they have experienced genuine spiritual conversion.

If we are in Christ, we have the grace of God in our lives—and we can use that grace to direct our tongue, so that we may bring honor and glory to God. If, however, we continuously live with an uncontrolled tongue, it is indicative of the fact that we are not truly in Christ. In other words, we can't truly be in Christ if we consistently slander others and tell lies. We should be alarmed if we do not sense an overwhelming conviction about such sinful behavior in our lives—conviction which the Holy Spirit promises to bring in the lives of all true believers.

The Inclination of the Tongue

Finally, in our passage, we should also see the inclination of the tongue, which is sinful. In verse 5, James warns, "So also the tongue is a small member, yet it boasts of great things." In our speech, as in all areas of our lives, we are naturally inclined to sin. We have a tendency to curse God and to sin against other people by the things that we say. The tongue is small, but it is powerfully dangerous, like a poisonous snake that can bite.

With our tongues, we can destroy churches; we can ruin families; we can divide brother against brother and sister against sister. Evil words can emotionally wound a spouse or provoke our children to anger. A person's character can be publicly shattered by what he says, or by what others might say about him.

So much of the evil and suffering in the world begins with sinful talk. Truly, the tongue can destroy our lives if we are not careful to honor God with how we use it. Regarding our ongoing struggle to guard our speech in this way, Matthew Henry wisely noted, "No man can tame the tongue without Divine grace and assistance. The apostle does not represent it as impossible, but as extremely difficult."[4] How true this is. Why don't we humbly pray to God to help us tame our tongues?

Study Questions

1. Why is it foolish to deny the universal truth about the tongue? Explain James's line of reasoning to answer this question.

2. In what area or sphere of your life are you most tempted to sin with your tongue? What steps of confession and repentance need to be taken?

---

4. Matthew Henry, *Short Comments on Every Chapter of the Holy Bible* (London: Religious Tract Society, 1839), 972.

3. In what way is your tongue important to the direction of your life? Explain the illustrations James uses to emphasize the importance of the tongue.

4. What are some practical and specific ways you can use your tongue to direct your life for God's glory?

5. Do you experience the Holy Spirit's conviction when you sin with your tongue? Why is your answer to this question so critical?

Chapter 4

Seven Descriptions of the Tongue

> How great a forest is set ablaze by such a small fire! And the tongue is a fire, a world of unrighteousness. The tongue is set among our members, staining the whole body, setting on fire the entire course of life, and set on fire by hell. For every kind of beast and bird, of reptile and sea creature, can be tamed and has been tamed by mankind, but no human being can tame the tongue. It is a restless evil, full of deadly poison.
> —James 3:5b–8

There is no denying that the tongue is a crucial part of the human body. There are at least four important roles that it plays in our daily lives. First, it helps us taste the food that we eat, notifying us of whether our food is too sour, too salty, or too hot to be eaten. Second, it enables us to chew and swallow food, so that our body may benefit from the food and our hunger may be satisfied. Third, it helps form the words and sounds required for speech. Fourth, it can also be used to discern if we are in good physical health.

When visiting the doctor's office, it is not uncommon to be told to "stick out your tongue." By looking at our tongue, the doctor can begin to determine whether more might be wrong with us. Virtually the same is true in a spiritual sense: the things that we say and the ways that we say them can reveal a great deal pertaining to the true health of our soul. None of us are in perfect health, though, for, as Karen Mains observed, "in the end our tongues always betray symptoms of soul sickness."[1]

In this chapter, we will emphasize seven critical things that our passage has to say about the tongue. So, let's consider these seven descriptions of the tongue one by one.

The Tongue Is a Fire (vv. 5b–6)

Our text begins, "How great a forest is set ablaze by such a small fire! And the tongue is a fire." Figuratively speaking, our tongue is like a small fire which can set an entire forest ablaze. This reminds me of a recent wildfire in Southern California that grew so large that several buildings were destroyed and around six thousand people had to evacuate the area. As hard as it is to believe, that massive fire which caused so much destruction started with a single flame.

James compares our tongues with a small fire, just like the one in California, which has destructive potential and can quickly lead to devastating results. Proverbs 16:27 echoes this same warning by declaring that the speech of a worthless man "is like a scorching fire." In fact, if even we, the people of God, cannot learn to control our tongues as Scripture calls us to do, then entire congregations, communities, and even nations are sure to be burned by the spiritual wildfires that will ensue.

---

1. *The Complete Guide to Christian Quotations* (Uhrichsville, OH: Barbour, 2011), 446.

The Tongue Is "a World of Unrighteousness" (v. 6)

Our tongues are like small "worlds" where all kinds of evil and unrighteousness reside. In places like this, slander, blasphemy, falsehood, gossip, and arrogant boasting are all practiced regularly. When we knowingly lie, the deception comes from us and from our own tongues—not from anyone else whom we might wish to blame. In fact, there are at least three different ways that we are prone to telling lies.

First (and perhaps most obvious), we lie to other people when we do not tell the truth. Children lie to their parents. Employees lie to their employers. Some people lie to their government officials as they file their taxes each year, and in turn, we suspect that the government sometimes deceives us by not disclosing the full truth about certain things. In all of these ways, great damage is done, and the consequences can easily become devastating.

Second, we also lie to ourselves. If we fail to acknowledge who we really are before God—according to His Word—then we are deceiving ourselves. Scripture makes it plain that we are sinners who are in desperate, continual need for God's grace. How foolish it is to attempt to deny this and to convince ourselves that we are good enough to enter heaven on our own merits. At the same time, we should be careful not to deceive ourselves into thinking that we are truly saved if, in fact, we are not, for as 1 John 2:4 states, "Whoever says 'I know him' but does not keep his commandments is a liar, and the truth is not in him."

Third, as we lie to others and to ourselves, we are also likely to lie to God. In doing this, we are disobeying God's law directly to His face. How foolish it is to say things that are not true to the one who knows all things far better than we do! This is the supreme demonstration of human arrogance.

Telling lies about God is just as wicked, and 1 John 2:22 makes this clear by asking, "Who is the liar but he who denies that Jesus is the Christ?" Anyone who denies Jesus Christ is a liar. As you might imagine, God takes this kind of sin most seriously. Consider the words of Proverbs 6:16–19: "There are six things that the Lord hates, seven that are an abomination to him: haughty eyes, a lying tongue, and hands that shed innocent blood, a heart that devises wicked plans, feet that make haste to run to evil, a false witness who breathes out lies, and one who sows discord among brothers."

Truly, God hates a lying tongue!

Some may try to argue that the best way to keep from lying and offending God is to be quiet. However, in certain situations, we can lie with our tongue just as obviously by silencing it. Proverbs 10:18 has this in mind when it declares, "The one who conceals hatred has lying lips, and whoever utters slander is a fool." We typically refer to this kind of sin as "silent abuse," or as giving somebody "the silent treatment." Examples of this sin include times when a husband and wife refuse to speak to one another because of an argument they had, or a parent is not talking to a troublesome child. In our churches, this behavior can also be seen when members who are at odds with one another refuse to pursue reconciliation with one another.

Are there any of us who are abusively silencing our tongue in this way? If so, we must urgently repent and seek God's forgiveness. God despises a lying tongue, and He declares that speech (or silence) of this sort is a "world of unrighteousness."

The Tongue "Stain[s] the Whole Body" (v. 6)

Sinful speech can stain your personality in the eyes of others. It can defile your character—sometimes in permanent and irreversible ways. In some situations, "sorry" is not enough to undo the pain that you have already caused others, and the way that the injured person sees you may be forever changed as a result.

There is a story about a little girl who went to her mother and said, "Which is worse, Momma—to lie or to steal?", to which the mother replied, "Both are sinful. I can't tell you which is worse."

The little girl sheepishly said, "Well, Momma, I've been thinking a good deal about it, and I think that lying is so much worse than stealing."

"Why, my child?" came the mother's reply.

"Well, because if you steal something, you can always take it back, unless you've eaten it—and if you've eaten it, you can pay for it—but a lie is forever."[2]

There is some truth to the girl's explanation. This kind of sin can stain us in significant ways and can make us desperately wish that we could retract some words that were spoken in the past. This is precisely why, earlier in the Book of James, we are told, "Religion that is pure and undefiled before God, the Father, is this: to visit orphans and widows in their affliction, and to keep oneself unstained from the world" (James 1:27).

We are all likely to be familiar with the famous nursery rhyme, "Sticks and stones may break my bones, but words

---

2. I owe this illustration to Spiros Zodhiates, comp., *Illustrations of Bible Truths* (Chattanooga, TN: AMG Publishers, 1991), 274.

will never hurt me." However, these words are not true. Words can hurt us deeply. In fact, sometimes it hurts us so badly that it can take a significant period of time for our emotional wound to heal. Let's seek to avoid being stained in such a way because of the words that we say.

The Tongue "Set[s] on Fire the Entire Course of Life" (v. 6)

This strong phrase can be difficult to understand, but I appreciate the way that Albert Barnes explains it, by saying, "The idea here is, that that which causes the tongue to do so much evil derives its origin from hell."[3] In a similar way, the Easy-to-Read Version of the Bible translates this passage as follows: "The tongue is like a fire. It is a world of evil among the parts of our body. It spreads its evil through our whole body and starts a fire that influences all of life. It gets this fire from hell."

So, we should recognize that an ungodly tongue acts as a fire and that this fire comes from hell. In other words, the power that our tongue possesses to destroy lives, damage communities, and harm our churches and even ourselves comes from hell. It comes from Satan, because the word *hell* in this passage comes from the Greek word *gehenna*, which means "the place of the devil." To state it another way, a lying tongue comes from the devil, who is both "a liar and the father of lies" (John 8:44).

---

3. Albert Barnes, *Notes, Explanatory and Practical on the General Epistles of James, Peter, John and Jude* (New York: Harper & Brothers, 1850), 67.

The Tongue Is Untamable (vv. 7–8a)

Generally speaking, even wild animals such as lions, tigers, elephants, birds, and snakes can all be tamed by people who have the skills to do that. In fact, it can be amazing to visit the circus or a theme park and watch trainers perform with the animals that they have trained. The Bible declares that God has given us dominion over the animals (Gen. 1:26, 28). Yet, Scripture also reminds us that while we may train the animals, nobody is able to tame their own tongue. We have no natural power to control our tongue. In fact, this is our biggest problem with regard to our tongue—we cannot tame it!

There are at least three reasons why this is so. First, as we have already seen, our tongue is like a wildfire that can burn out of control. The fire can burn so big that we cannot even begin to extinguish it ourselves.

Second, the fire comes from hell and from the devil himself. In our own strength, we are no match for Satan. Satan is powerful, but, praise be to God, "He who is in you is greater than he who is in the world" (1 John 4:4). James makes it clear that while we cannot defeat the devil ourselves, we can trust in God and in His Holy Spirit who dwells within every believer, and we can be confident that in Christ, we have eternal victory over sin and the consequences of sin.

Third, as both James 3:2 and Romans 3:23 remind us, none of us are perfect. In our sinful imperfection, we are not nearly capable of defeating the sin in our lives, but our perfect God is capable of overcoming sin, and we can trust in Him fully.

The Tongue Is a "Restless Evil" (v. 8b)

This same description is given to the devil himself in 1 Peter 5:8, which declares that "your adversary the devil prowls around like a roaring lion, seeking someone to devour." Satan is a restless evil. He is active. He is not lazy but is always working, trying to deceive and confuse as many people as he possibly can. In the same way, sinful speech intends to deceive its listeners and to keep them away from the truth. The natural tendency of the tongue is toward sin, but God calls us to fight against this tendency by coming to Him and by allowing Him to redeem our speech for His glory in ways that we could never do apart from Him.

The Tongue Is "Full of Deadly Poison" (v. 8c)

Here, James portrays the tongue as that of a poisonous snake. Psalm 140:3 explains, "Their tongues are like deadly snakes; their words are like a cobra's poison." Also, Proverbs 11:9 warns us that "with his mouth the godless man would destroy his neighbor." Figuratively speaking, our tongues are filled with poison and have great potential to harm others. Ungodly speech is filled with venom and can poison those whom it seeks to harm as if it were a deadly snake.

After considering all of the ways that the tongue can harm others and ourselves, how should we respond? I have two helpful suggestions to offer. First, let us be more gracious to each other. We must be quick to forgive and to seek forgiveness from others. If your goal is to find mistakes, then you will easily find some, since we are all sinful and imperfect. However, before you condemn others for mistakes that they have made, it would be wise to remind yourself that you have similar tendencies in your own life.

In Ephesians 4:29, Paul instructs us to "let no corrupting talk come out of your mouths, but only such as is good for building up, as fits the occasion, that it may give grace to those who hear" (Eph. 4:29). Strive to speak to others in love, and to use words which will edify and bless rather than harm.

First Peter 4:8 exhorts, "Above all, keep loving one another earnestly, since love covers a multitude of sins." Are you gracious to others, or do you seek to be so critical of others? Peter reminds us, though, that if we truly love others, that love will cover a multitude of sins. This does not mean that we will be tolerating the sins of others, but rather that we grow in patience, understanding, and love as we increasingly seek to demonstrate God's love to others–that divine love which He has so graciously shown to us.

Second, let us learn more about our tongue. We must continue reflecting on what God's Word says about our tongue, especially in regard to how we can tame it with God's help. James explains to us that if we cannot control our tongues, we can't control the other parts of our bodies either. How wonderful it would be then to progressively be able to control the use of our tongues in such a way that God is honored and people are blessed. We should prayerfully desire to do this.

The Puritan Thomas Watson famously wrote, "God has given us two ears, but one tongue, to show that we should be swift to hear, but slow to speak. God has set a double fence before the tongue, the teeth, and the lips, to teach us to be wary that we offend not with our tongue."[4] Oh, may God help us to utilize our tongues for His glory and for the good of others!

Study Questions

1. Can you think of practical examples in which the tongue has been like a fire? Has your tongue ever caused a wildfire?

2. What are the three ways in which we are prone to tell lies? Ask the Holy Spirit to show you in which area your tongue has been or is a "world of unrighteousness."

3. Where does the tongue's power to destroy come from? How can understanding the answer to this question help us resist the temptation to use our tongues for evil?

4. How did Christ resist Satan's temptation to use His tongue for evil? Take a moment to praise and thank Christ for His perfect obedience.

5. Why is it important to strive, by God's grace, to control our tongues? What steps, if any, have you taken to do this?

---

4. Thomas Watson, *A Body of Divinity* (1692; repr., London: Banner of Truth Trust, 1965), 115.

Chapter 5

The Inconsistency of the Tongue

With it [the tongue] we bless our Lord and Father, and with it we curse people who are made in the likeness of God. From the same mouth come blessing and cursing. My brothers, these things ought not to be so. Does a spring pour forth from the same opening both fresh and salt water? Can a fig tree, my brothers, bear olives, or a grapevine produce figs? Neither can a salt pond yield fresh water. —James 3:9–12

According to one Japanese proverb, "The tongue is but three inches long, yet it can kill a man six feet high."[1] How true it is that words have great potential to change our lives forever. One reason that this is so is because we use our words to accomplish so many different things. With the same mouth, we pronounce both words of blessing and words of cursing. God's Word, however, exhorts us to be consistent in our speech. Just as we seek to honor God consistently with our thinking and feelings, so we must also seek to honor God with our speaking. As in every other area of Christian growth, though, to be consistent with our tongues takes some work. So, let's look more closely at this passage and

---

1. Tyron Edwards, *A Dictionary of Thoughts: Being a Cyclopedia of Laconic Quotations from the Best Authors, Both Ancient and Modern* (New York: Cassell Publishing Company, 1891), 579.

consider how we might be able to submit this area of our lives to God more fully.

Our Tongues Are Inconsistent (v. 9)

Our text begins by saying, "With it we bless our Lord and Father." Here the tongue is depicted as an instrument through which we bless our God. Of course, other parts of our bodies should also be used for blessing the Lord. Our eyes, ears, hands, and feet—our entire bodies should be utilized as instruments through which we bless God. Yet, in this passage James is specifically reminding us to employ our tongues as instruments of blessing God.

Is it not interesting that, in verse 9, it is *we* who are said to do the blessing? After all, we should all recognize the fact that God is the greatest source of blessing, and that it is usually God whom the Bible describes as blessing others. That's why we pray on a daily basis, "Lord, please bless us." However, in this verse, we see James telling us that we can use our tongues to bless our Lord. It is rather humbling to think that we can bless the God who created us, but what exactly does this mean?

The Bible uses the word *bless* in three distinct ways. First, it is used to bestow grace. Ephesians 1:3 demonstrates this usage with the pronouncement, "Blessed be the God and Father of our Lord Jesus Christ, who has blessed us in Christ with every spiritual blessing in the heavenly places." In this context, "bless" means to bestow grace, and only God can do that.

Second, the word *bless* may also be used to ask God to bestow His grace on others. For example, in Luke 6:23, Jesus instructs His disciples to "bless those who curse you, pray for those who abuse you." In this case, the disciples of Jesus are told to bless their persecutors, and to do so primarily by praying and asking God to bestow His blessings upon the persecutors. Even when we are despised by others, we should pray for them as Jesus taught us to do.

Third, the term *bless* may also be used to describe our praise of God. We praise Him when we acknowledge who He is and what He has done for us in Christ. It is in this context that James is using the word *bless*. Psalm 103:1–3 uses the word *bless* in the same way: "Bless the LORD, O my soul, and all that is within me, bless his holy name! Bless the LORD, O my soul, and forget not all his benefits, who forgives all your iniquity." In what way does David want his soul to "bless the LORD"? He is exhorting his soul to bless the Lord with worship, praise, and adoration as a fitting response to all that God has done for him.

As James reminds us, we are able to bless the Lord in this way, as an act of worship, with our tongues. When we worship God as a church family, that's exactly what we do. We speak our prayers to God; we sing songs of praise; we respond to His Word; we edify one another; and in all of these ways, we are blessing God with our words.

Nevertheless, James explains that there is a great irony in our behavior which is in desperate need of correction, for with that very same tongue that we use to bless God, we also curse people. The word *curse*, like the word *bless*, can be used in different ways. First, it can mean to make something useless. Though humans are certainly capable of destroying things, the word *curse* is used in this way to describe an ability which only God has. For example, in Mark 11, Jesus curses a fig tree, saying, "May no one ever eat fruit from you again." Jesus declares the tree to be cursed, and it is.

James, however, uses the word *curse* in another way: to mean wishing evil to happen to others. This is a sad truth: with the same tongue with which we bless God, we also speak hateful things to (or about) other people. We may not have the ability to cause terrible things to happen to others, but that does not prevent us from using our tongues to wish it were so. What a terrible sin this is—and how frequently it is committed by those who claim to follow Christ.

Notice, though, that James includes himself in this sinful confession, by saying, "we bless our Lord and Father" and "we curse people." Why does James include himself? James could be speaking "as the representative of his people in the name of his guilty people."[2] This is very similar to when I am preaching a sermon and say something like, "Unbelievers, *we* must believe in the Lord Jesus Christ or else we will remain under God's wrath!" Obviously, by God's grace I am already a believer in Christ, but I will still sometimes speak to you as a representative of those within our congregation, or those present in a worship service, who do not yet trust in Christ.

Again, verse 9 shows us the great inconsistency in how we use our tongues, and verse 10 states it even more plainly: "From the same mouth come blessing and cursing." In Psalm 62:4, David describes the enemies of God in a similar way: "They take pleasure in falsehood. They bless with their mouths, but inwardly they curse." In other words, they are

---

2. John Peter Lange, *A Commentary on the Holy Scriptures: Critical, Doctrinal, and Homiletical, With Special Reference to Ministers and Students* (New York: Charles Scribner's Sons, 1900), 99.

hypocrites. When those outside of the church complain about hypocrites, who speak lovingly about God but hatefully about other people, could it possibly be you or I whom they are thinking of? Let's hope not! In any case, this passage goes on to offer us God-honoring instruction about how we may change this behavior in our lives.

God Commands Us to Be Consistent with Our Tongues (v. 10b)

The passage continues, "My brothers, these things ought not to be so." This passionate appeal is addressed to "brothers," those who profess to follow Christ. There is urgency in these words, and they are intended to convey the idea that this sinful behavior of cursing is not necessary, beneficial, or edifying to anyone. James is saying, "Stop doing this. It is disobedience to God!"

The previous verse offers a compelling reason why this is so: because the curses are directed toward "people who are made in the likeness of God." Do you know why we should not curse even unbelievers—even radical Muslims who despise us? Because they, too, were created in the image of God. That's why James uses the generic term for "people" (*anthropos* in the original Greek), which means men, women, boys, and girls of every religion and nationality. All of us were created in God's image (Gen. 1:26). This is why James exhorts us to not curse others with our speech. To curse the image-bearers of God is to also curse the God whose image they bear.

Paul exhorts us in Romans 12:14, "Bless those who persecute you; bless and do not curse them." We are told not to say evil words about our persecutors, but, oh, how easy it is to sin in this way . . . especially when we read news reports about the worldwide persecution of our brothers and sisters in Christ.

In one news report, al-Qaeda-linked rebels seized control of a Christian village in Syria. One resident of that village who was a Christian man said that the militants were forcing his fellow Christians to convert to Islam. In his words, "I saw the militants grabbing five villagers Wednesday and threatening them [saying]: 'Either you convert to Islam, or you will be beheaded.'"[3] By reports like this, we almost cannot help but become very angry and pronounce a curse on these persecutors, because the injustice of the situation grieves our hearts terribly.

Still another troubling report tells of a Christian mother who was fined a month's average salary because of her nine-year-old son's "illegal religious activity" at school. Her son, David, had given audio CDs to his two teachers as gifts. When the school's head teacher saw the label "God loves you too" on one of the CDs, she immediately contacted the police. An investigator asked the boy who permitted him to bring these CDs to school. The boy replied, "My mother," and his mother was then fined for having allowed her son to do this.[4]

How fascinating it is that, in this case, the CD title "God loves you too" was instantly understood to be a reference to the God of the Bible. Isn't it encouraging for us to know that

---

3. "Al Qaeda-Linked Rebels Gain Control of Christian Village, Syrian Activists Say," *Fox News*, September 8, 2013, http://www.foxnews.com/world/2013/09/08/syrian-activists-say-al-qaida-linked-rebels-gain-control-christian-village.html (accessed June 27, 2016).
4. "Kazakh Baptists Fined for Worship Meetings," *Baptist Press*, August 27, 2013, http://www.bpnews.net/40979 (accessed June 27, 2016).

our God—the only true God—is the God of love, and that even non-believers recognize that? Shouldn't "Allah" also be acknowledged to be a god who loves his people? Yet, in this case, the CD was not identified in such a way. This, too, tends to anger us because of the terrible injustice shown toward followers of Christ. Yet, we must remember to conform ourselves to the teaching of God's Word, which tells us not to speak evil against others—even those who wish to do evil to us—because they, too, were created in the image of God.

James Illustrates the Need for Us to Be Consistent with Our Tongues (v. 11)

Again, our text reads: "Does a spring pour forth from the same opening both fresh and salt water?" Or, more literally, does the fountain out of the same opening pour forth both the sweet (blessing) and the bitter (cursing) water? The obvious answer, of course, is "No, of course not. This is impossible."

As you likely know, Israel has many fountains of water, which, when they are full, will burst forth with water and provide a source of fresh flowing water for the streams and brooks. In effect, James is reminding his readers to not expect to have two different kinds of water flowing from the same source, since that would be contrary to God's design in nature. In a similar way, it is morally contrary to God's law for us to use our tongues to both bless God and curse other people. We can't do this.

James may also be echoing the words of his half-brother, the Lord Jesus Christ, who in Luke 6:45 said, "The good person out of the good treasure of his heart produces good, and the evil person out of his evil treasure produces evil, for out of the abundance of the heart his mouth speaks." Here, the human heart is shown to be similar to the fountains of Israel, for when the heart is full, it produces words which flow out of the mouth.

In other words, the speech that we produce is an excellent indicator of what is in our hearts. That being the case, our biggest problem is not our tongue but the condition of our hearts, from which our speech truly comes. J. C. Ryle explains, "Our words are the evidence of the state of our hearts, as surely as the taste of the water is an evidence of the state of the spring."[5]

Lately, my wife and I have been reading Tedd Tripp's book, *Shepherding a Child's Heart*, and he makes this same biblical observation there. When a child says something bad, the real problem is not the child's tongue but his heart, which is "deceitful above all things and beyond cure" (Jer. 17:9).[6] We know that only God can cure and change a heart like this.

I suspect that when the original readers of the book of James first received this book and came upon verse 11, describing the different kinds of water that might pour forth from a spring, they likely reflected on one particular event that had taken place many years prior to that time. Here's the account of the event, as recorded in Exodus 15:22–25:

> Then Moses made Israel set out from the Red Sea, and they went into the wilderness of Shur. They went three days in the wilderness and found no water. When they came to Marah, they could not drink the water of Marah because it was bitter; therefore it was named Marah. And the people grumbled against Moses, saying, "What shall we drink?" And he cried to the LORD, and the LORD showed

5. J. C. Ryle, *Expository Thoughts on the Gospels* (New York: Robert Carter & Bothers, 1860), 133.
6. New International Version.

him a log, and He threw it into the water, and the water became sweet.

Some commentators understand the wooden log to represent symbolically the cross of our Lord Jesus Christ, because it made the bitter waters sweet. We recognize that only the cross of Christ can make our bitter tongues sweet again—and only the cross can make our sinful hearts pure. In fact, without the cross of Christ, there would be nothing that we could do to address sufficiently the sin problem in our lives. However, we can give thanks to God, for the gospel of Jesus Christ is absolutely true, and through Him our hearts may be eternally changed.

So, I urge you to consider the cross of Christ every day as you seek to honor God with your life. When we wake up in the morning, we should remember that we have this awful tendency to be inconsistent in how we use our tongues and acknowledge that before God. We should all pray, "Lord, help me to resist sin," and remind ourselves of our desperate need for the gospel. Without the gospel of Jesus Christ, we would continue to use our tongues for evil purposes, but because of our relationship with Christ, we can both honor God and bless others with our words.

Some may try to argue, "I was born this way, and I can't really control the things I say." In regard to your own abilities, you are absolutely right. We can't make ourselves resist sin on our own. The solution, though, is the gospel of Jesus Christ.

James uses two more illustrations to express these profound truths to us, writing in 3:12, "Can a fig tree, my brothers, bear olives, or a grapevine produce figs? Neither can a salt pond yield fresh water." The point, again, is that we should be consistent in the ways that we use our tongues.

Obviously, the issue of hypocrisy is closely connected to the problem that James is addressing in this text. The same call to consistent, righteous living is also issued to us by our Lord, who taught the following to His disciples in Matthew 6:24: "No one can serve two masters, for either he will hate the one and love the other, or he will be devoted to the one and despise the other. You cannot serve God and money."

We cannot truthfully say "I love Jesus" if our lives do not reflect that claim. And we are not entitled to sing "I love to tell the story" if we are ignoring what the song says. It is one thing to *say* these things but another thing to *do* them. Nonetheless, if we want to avoid being appropriately labeled as "hypocrites," our words and our actions must be in obvious alignment. May the Lord help us to use our tongues wisely and consistently, so that, through our speech, He may be truly exalted in our lives.

Study Questions

1. How does James use the word *bless* in our passage?

2. In what way can we bless the Lord with our tongues?

3. How can the same tongue that blesses God also engage in cursing? Have you been guilty of this inconsistency? If so, how?

4. What compelling reason does James give to stop cursing others?

5. How does the use of your tongue indicate what is in your heart?

6. How and why is the gospel of Christ the solution to the problem we have with our tongues?

Afterword

In this booklet, Pastor Brian Najapfour has riveted our attention on a crucial component of the Christian life: the use of the tongue. In a scriptural and compelling way, he develops the argument that the sinful use of the tongue is a prevalent sin among professing Christians. How convicting it is to read of the various ways in which we are all guilty of using our tongues as instruments of sin rather than of righteousness.

Pastor Najapfour makes an equally compelling case that when we use our tongues as instruments of sin, we discredit not only our Christian profession but also the Christ whom we are called to represent in this world. He therefore argues that the proper use of our tongues is a crucial and non-negotiable component of a sanctified life. In fact, he goes so far as to say that anyone who professes to be a Christian and yet consistently abuses his or her tongue may very well prove to be a self-deceived soul. In other words, when the Holy Spirit regenerates us and makes us new creatures in Christ (2 Cor. 5:18), he will also sanctify our tongues.

And indeed, the sanctification of the tongue is an essential ingredient of the sanctification of the entire man. An important aspect of sanctification is that the Holy Spirit progressively causes us to begin to answer to the purpose for which we were created: to know, love, magnify, and serve our Creator. God created us with a tongue for the purpose of worshiping him verbally; that is, to express vocally our love and adoration for the God who created us in the image of his Son. The fall of man dramatically and tragically corrupted this wonderful instrument of worship, having now become an instrument—as James puts it—that "is set on fire of hell" (James 3:6).

Pastor Najapfour emphasizes throughout this booklet that all of this corrupt tendency changes when the Spirit of God renews us and begins to conform us to the image of God's Son. Our tongues will again begin to answer to the purpose for which they were created: to worship and adore God. In fact, the sanctified use of the tongue will be such that also in our speaking, we begin to resemble Christ. Of Christ we read, "Never man spake like this man" (John 7:46). In some sense this ought to be true of the Christian as well. As Pastor Najapfour has pointed out, just as the accent of one who is not a native speaker will identify his or her ethnic origin, so must the Christian speak with a heavenly accent. That accent should be evident to all with whom we providentially interact. It should be said of us what was said to Peter in the hall of Caiaphas: "Surely thou art also one of them; for thy speech betrayeth thee" (Matt. 26:73).

Pastor Najapfour compels us to come to grips with the question whether as professing Christians we truly speak with a Christian accent, thereby bringing honor to the Christ whom we profess to love and serve. Pastor Najapfour underscores this by going to considerable length in expounding the sobering warning of James when he writes, "If any man among you seem to be religious, and bridleth not his tongue, but deceiveth his own heart, this man's religion is vain" (James 1:26).

May God therefore bless the reading of this much needed treatise regarding the Christian's use of the tongue! May it prompt us to examine ourselves prayerfully in *coram Deo* regarding our use of the tongue, praying with David, "Search me, O God, and know my heart: try me, and know my thoughts: and see if there be any wicked way in me, and lead me in the way everlasting" (Ps. 139:23–24). And may the fruit of such self-examination be that we will daily heed the exhortation of the apostle Paul, "Let your speech be alway with grace, seasoned with salt, that ye may know how ye ought to answer every man" (Col. 4:6).

Rev. Bartel Elshout
Heritage Reformed Congregation
Hull, Iowa

About the Author

Born and reared in the Philippines, **Brian G. Najapfour** has been a minister of God since 2001. Called to the gospel ministry at the young age of sixteen, he began his theological education in 1997 at the Center for Biblical Studies Institute and Seminary in the Philippines. There, with God's help, he earned his Bachelor of Theology (B.Th.) degree in 2001, followed by his Master in Biblical Studies (M.B.S.) degree in 2004. From 2001 until his coming to the U.S. in 2006, he served as a pastor in the Philippines. With a desire to further his education, however, he arrived in Grand Rapids, Michigan, in 2006, where he enrolled in Puritan Reformed Theological Seminary. There, he studied for his Master of Theology (Th.M.) degree, which he completed by God's grace in 2009.

While pursuing a Ph.D. degree, Najapfour, since his installation on October 19, 2012, has been the pastor of Dutton United Reformed Church in Caledonia, Michigan. He is co-editor (along with Joel R. Beeke) of *Taking Hold of God: Reformed and Puritan Perspectives on Prayer* (2011) and author of *The Very Heart of Prayer: Reclaiming John Bunyan's Spirituality* (2012), *Jonathan Edwards: His Doctrine of and Devotion to Prayer* (2013), and *Child Dedication: Considered Historically, Theologically, and Pastorally* (2014).

He and his wife, Sarah, have three children, Anna, James, and Abigail. For more information about him, visit his website: biblicalspiritualitypress.org

Note to the Reader

The publisher invites you to respond to us about this book by writing to Reformed Fellowship, Inc., at *president@ reformedfellowship.net*

Founded in 1951, Reformed Fellowship, Inc., is a religious and strictly nonprofit organization composed of a group of Christian believers who hold to the biblical Reformed faith. Our purpose is to advocate and propagate this faith, to nurture those who seek to live in obedience to it, to give sharpened expression to it, to stimulate the doctrinal sensitivities of those who profess it, to promote the spiritual welfare and purity of the Reformed churches, and to encourage Christian action.

Members of Reformed Fellowship express their adherence to the Calvinistic creeds as formulated in the *Belgic Confession*, the *Heidelberg Catechism*, the *Canons of Dort*, and the *Westminster Confession and Catechisms*.

To fulfill our mission, we publish a bimonthly journal, *The Outlook*, and we publish books and Bible study guides. Our website is *www.reformedfellowship.net*.